D1491086

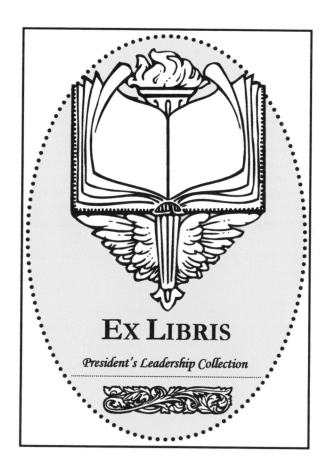

EX LIBRIS

President's Leadership Collection

RIGHT MAKES MIGHT

Reviving Ethics to Improve Your Business

Dorothea E. Gaulden, PhD

Edit by
Dr. Sharon Brown

RIGHT MAKES MIGHT: REVIVING ETHICS TO IMPROVE YOUR BUSINESS
PUBLISHED BY BRIDGEWAY BOOKS
P.O. BOX 80107
AUSTIN, TEXAS 78758

For more information about our books, please write to us, call 512.478.2028, or visit our website at www.bridgewaybooks.net.

Library of Congress Control Number: 2006940667

ISBN-13: 978-1-933538-86-0
ISBN-10: 1-933538-86-4

Donation
Dr. Scott

DEDICATION

I dedicate this Christ-driven manifestation, which reflects my sincere desire to be part of an ethical revival in our business community, to my loving family—my husband, daughters, and grandchildren.

ACKNOWLEDGEMENTS

Without Christ, this effort could not have been accomplished. His awesome guidance, which steered me through the maze, permitted me the opportunity to present an open discussion on how ethical behavior, once a key element in the fabric of our lives, is now at best just another debatable topic. Leaning on His Word and not my might or power, I was given the courage to tackle this horrendous endeavor (Zechariah 4:6).

TABLE OF CONTENTS

PREFACE

Do not confuse motion and progress. A rocking horse keeps moving but does not make any progress.

Alfred A. Montapert

My career as a finance executive in the corporate business environment was one of excitement, even though normal business challenges—such as striving to maximize the wealth of our shareholders or adhering to proper and ethical financial reporting—often clouded my portfolio of never-ending tasks. While demanding, my chosen livelihood gave me the opportunity to realize one of my passions—love for the business community. I was ecstatic to be associated with the finance discipline and the great American business community; it provided me an opportunity to actively participate in bettering our society through quality products, socialization, and contributions to humanity. Nevertheless, after spending many exciting and productive years as a finance executive, and most recently experiencing adjunct business professorship, I am greatly troubled by the unethical behavior flourishing both in our business community and, particularly, our classrooms—the training ground for future leaders.

This obvious lack of adherence to established common sense, respect for others, and the willingness of both the business community and individuals to blatantly engage in practices such as embezzlement, fraudulent misrepresentations, and cheating cannot be minimized. As noted by ever-present media accounts, families are destroyed and businesses lose credibility. Some must file for bankruptcy, leading to shattered dreams and the elimination of jobs that are necessary to maintain a healthy economic base in America. Without a doubt, morally depraved actions render grave consequences to everyone. They are costly, not only in absolute financial terms, but because they feed into a continuing spiral of moral decay. In addition, these unacceptable acts widen the gulf between individuals and business entities; this diminishes a needed ingredient in all transactions—trust. Guess who bears the cost? You, the consumer!

In all likelihood you are thinking, why another book about ethics? There are hundreds, if not thousands, of volumes debating, admonishing, or even dispelling the entire notion that ethics is a reliable concept. However my desire in authoring this book is not to debate or even dispel ethics, but to explore the need to understand the tremendous impact unethical behavior has on the business community; its burden, financially and morally, on society; and lastly, to offer a workable remedy for the contagious disease that ravishes our business community. Similar to going to one's personal physician, without a therapeutic solution, a diagnosis yields only one bleak choice: either you accept and remain in a "status quo" position or get worse. Can America afford to stay in a diagnostic stage? In other words, remain in a "status quo" position, which most likely will only get worse. Is it even a choice? Astonishing what Abraham Lincoln thought:

America will never be destroyed from the outside. If we falter and lose our freedoms, it will be because we destroyed ourselves.

CHAPTER 1
STAGING GROUND

Without civic morality communities perish; without personal morality their survival has no value.

Bertrand Russell

During my high school days, biology students were obligated to dissect defenseless frogs under the premise that by so doing the student would have a better understanding of the frog. Aside from causing a queasy stomach for some, the investigative surgery afforded students the opportunity to gain valuable insight into the complex inner-workings of the web-footed, primarily aquatic amphibian. Similar to uncovering the frog's inner workings in order to gain valuable insight, man's inquisitiveness has revealed that to better understand business ethics (i.e., ethical behavior in the business community) it has to be viewed from two aspects: individual ethical astuteness and corporate ethical adaptableness. Although distinctively different, they have incredible influence on each other.

One of my grandsons loves to tell stories. The first thing he does is "set the stage." This usually entails great details, which can be initially quite boring, but ultimately you are drawn into the story by his vivid descriptions and animations. Making use of this learned behavior, I urge you to allow me a few moments of indulgence. First and foremost, in order to adequately explore the two aspects of business ethics we need to understand and accept the premise that the precise concept of ethics and morality is extremely complex.

Most individuals would immediately agree that ethics and morality are characteristically associated with values of good and bad, right and wrong, and how people should act. Although easily delineated when defining, they continue to be debated. For centuries intellectuals have argued questions such as, are ethics and morality totally objective phenomena or subjective? Do they originate from some supernatural being, or are they embedded within nature itself? Could ethics and morality be a product of the minds of human beings?[1]

When these thought-provoking questions are integrated as a sum total, it appears the outcome culminates into an overriding, threefold dilemma—how human beings should act, what acts should be done, and how should the acts be implemented? As to that, esteemed scholars have put forth numerous postulations. Some have concluded that the issue could best be answered by the religious or scientific community, or even through political action.[2] These friends of ours are asking us to put the ball in the scientific, religious, or political court. Let them be the gurus. On the other hand, Henry Sidgwick and other nineteenth-century intellects disagreed with this obvious attempt to dismiss the practical role of ethics and concluded that ethics could not be grounded in religion.[3] Their thinking culminated in uncertainty about how ethics might be put into practical use. In contrast, other ethicists during the nineteenth century believed that morality emanates from some higher supernatural being(s) or principles, which embody the highest good and reveal to individuals what is right or wrong, good or bad. Simply put, persons yearning to be ethical and moral adhere to a prescribed doctrine where disobedience is considered immoral and possibly exposes the believer to temporary or eternal punishment.[4]

Despite all of the academic studies, the countless written volumes, and the postulations, an aura still remains around ethics and morality. Some of the greatest minds have tackled the ethics and morality dilemma, yet none have arrived at a resolute consensus. Therefore, both intellectuals and religious practitioners continue to be challenged to seek answers that will explain why individuals choose to act either ethically or unethically with minimum thought about the consequences. Hooray! We are not as dumb as we thought we were.

Individual Ethics Astuteness

As water reflects a face, so a man's heart reflects the man.
Proverbs 27:19 NIV

It is only with the heart that one can see rightly; what is essential is invisible to the eye.

Antoine de Saint-Exupery

Reading the newspaper is an enjoyable daily ritual for my empty-nest household; besides debating and arguing, my husband and I courageously solve the world's problems without leaving the breakfast table. We also chuckle at a typical aspect of the reported "news," which is the conglomerate of descriptors tagged to the end of people's names, such as graduate of, married with, employed by, avid fan of, etc. These expressive descriptors allow the reader to interpret and paint a stunning picture of the situation and/or individual(s). This can be fun! Using a little imagination, the reader creates a personalized story, normally dotted with personal experience. This same principle applies to ethical discernment. The descriptors ascribed to ethical behavior propel the personal and artistic interpretation of ethical astuteness. In times gone by, individuals who exhibited honesty, fairness, loyalty, kindness, compassion, unselfishness, and courage were considered to behave ethically or morally. The family, religion, and the government shaped these idealistic values. Not so today! Nowadays, many Americans credit themselves with determining what practices are ethical or unethical.[5]

When this core transition occurred is not the key question. The true question is, does the transition accurately portray American society? If the answer is yes, and the assertion (individualized ethical usurpation) exemplifies reality, then we need to understand and ask the hard question: What, then, are the motivating factors that steer individuals to behave ethically? Benedict de Spinoza suggested that individuals are guided by nature and that virtuous individuals will ultimately seek to understand God's nature.[6] Therefore he purported that an individual's belief in God stimulates ethical behavior. In contrast Friedrich Nietzsche stated that being an atheist in of itself stimulates ethical behavior.[7] He purported that religion was harmful to human life, because it degraded the natural capacity for achievement. Nel Noddings further postulated that when individuals embrace a philosophy of caring, that alone drives the individual to act ethically.[8] These personal positions ranging from believing in God to atheism underscore the complexity of ethical behavior and the stimulus associated with the individual's choice to engage in wrongful practices.

Among the many organized institutions, the workplace appears to be a fertile breeding ground for wrongful practices.

Studies have shown that four common scenarios prompt individuals to make unethical behavior choices in the workplace. The first scenario is when employees encounter uncertainty about acceptable or appropriate behavior, which is born from ill-defined situations and ambiguous company expectations. The second scenario is when employees sense a duality between what the company says and what it really expects. Next, individuals are prompted to make unethical choices when they believe they are acting in the company's best interest, usually because the company condones the unethical action and rewards the individual. The last situation—unlike the first three, which were perceived to be for the betterment of the firm—is completely dominated by selfish ambition. The individual, to gain power, money, or advancement, willingly chooses to engage in unethical behavior.[9] Besides observing corrupt practices for selfish ambition or personal gain via the media, reliable statistics are readily available. For example when a group of individuals were instructed to identify examples of unethical behavior supported by their rationale, 74 percent cited more power, 73 percent more money, 46 percent faster advancement, and 38 percent cited more recognition.[10]

The sad thing about the contagious nature of unethical behavior is that it is has no boundaries. The virus goes beyond the work environment—it saturates society's tapestry, which includes institutions of higher education. As an adjunct university professor I am still amazed at the magnitude of unethical behavior I see in the form of cheating. During one academic session I observed fourteen offenses by seven students in a particular class. Regardless of the rationale for violating academic honesty, this warped picture in our learning institutions is real. Out of 207 graduate students, 80 percent confessed to committing at least one out of fifteen unethical academic practices frequently. The primary reason given was to get a better grade.

They believed their actions did not hurt others and the likelihood of being caught was slim.[11]

CORPORATE ETHICS ADAPTABLENESS

We have, in fact, two kinds of morality side by side: one, which we preach but do not practice, and another which we practice but seldom preach.

Bertrand Russell

God, in all His wisdom, graciously created mankind in His image and lovingly endowed him two arms. Physically, they appear as two separate and independent limbs, but contrary to observation, they have a common shoulder girdle—two bones, known as the clavicle and the scapula. The two bones working as a common girdle give great mobility and utility to the arms. This, too, can be said about business ethics and individual ethics. Although appearing as separate, unattached, dangling concepts, business ethics shares a common heritage with individual ethics.

Positionally, business ethics is on a sprouting journey. Philosophers, theologians, and various types of social scientists are heavily involved in exploring and expanding on the concept. Although its emergence is observable, history records a struggle for acceptance as a respectable field of study because of the hesitance of scholars to confront resistance from the business community in questioning long-established norms. Once totally off-limits, the ethical correctness of the business community is now a fundamental part of the academic instructional environment.

Claiming its rightful place as a crucial component—instructional in academia and behavioral in the business community—business ethics viewed comprehensively describes business life and its practices. It embodies an understanding and appreciation of fair play and camaraderie. It also involves an appreciation of those ambitions and goals over and above the profit motive, which requires paying attention to the details of the organization and not just the problems.[12] Conceptually, business ethics is a specialized area in which ethical issues, and a systematic approach to solving these issues, are very important. Operationally, it establishes and maintains crucial relationships among individuals in the organization where ethical principles (a) espouse the value of life, (b) strive for goodness while avoiding badness, (c) justly and fairly distribute good and bad, (d) encourage honesty and truth telling, and (e) respect individual freedom.[13]

These principles that embody general individual basic rights (right to life, justice, honesty and truth telling, privacy, and freedom) have been noted in numerous business directives, such as those promulgated by Pfizer and Lockheed Martin. For example, Pfizer Inc. advocates that to fulfill its purpose and mission, the company abides by eight principles that embrace integrity, respect for people, teamwork, performance, innovation, customer focus, leadership, and community. Pfizer considers these as foundational values. Similarly, Lockheed Martin includes honesty, integrity, respect, trust, responsibility, and citizenship in its ethical principle directive.[14]

Other indications of acceptance of business ethics as a discipline worthy of integration into the business community are illustrated by the formation of business centers that are engaged in a variety of business research and the expansion of endowed chairs. The publication of two business journals that specifically address business ethics, *Business and Professional Ethics* and the *Journal of Business Ethics*, also signal the acceptance of business ethics. The heightened awareness and acceptance of business ethics as a legitimate discipline has spawned research investigations at many societal and organizational levels. This, then, raises the question of moral agency—who or what is responsible for illegal acts within the organization?[15]

Moral agency—that is, what or who can be held accountable—has two schools of thought. The first thought is that firms are merely legal constructions with no rights or responsibility, while the second view advocates that firms act as full-fledged moral agents with moral rights and responsibilities. The latter view supports America's stance that corporations are artificial persons. As such, corporations can own property and have freedom of speech; therefore, corporations can engage in unethical behavior.[16]

Since corporations can be indicted or admonished for dishonorable actions, such as dumping of hazardous waste, sexual harassment, falsifying reports, and willfully using defective materials, they must constantly examine and address those potential pitfalls that ultimately lead to inexcusable deeds. Essentially the overriding task is to minimize the risk of unethical behavior through risk management. Within most organizations there are two directives that are intended to manage and minimize unacceptable behavior—standard operating procedures and a code of ethics. Although the purpose for both are to reduce unwarranted practices, research suggests that established standard operating procedures are highly suspect of contributing to illegal or criminal acts by encouraging individuals to commit crimes on behalf of the company.[17] Similarly, a code of ethics, contrary to belief, fails to minimize violations. The relationship between a code of ethics and corporate unethical violations is minimal.[18]

How wonderful life would be for the business community if it were possible to connect unethical corporate behavior to certain variables such as a code of ethics, standard operating procedures, industry characteristics, or profit performance. Nonetheless, if this connection were established, insight into these relationships would tell very little about the behavioral aspect inside the firm, of individuals, or even the industry. Without additional knowledge that spells out the behavioral stimuli that led to the illegal or unethical action, one can only guess why and under what circumstances the work environment, industry, or individual is correlated with criminal behavior.[19] When forty individuals in the work environment were studied, it became apparent that when faced with having to make choices that were morally conflicting, each individual's concept of morality resembled a tapestry of perceptions, experiences, values, and needs.[20] The choices were individualized in the corporate setting.

Just as individuals are guided by personal ethics when faced with moral dilemmas, enterprises also have a set of ethics that steer the firm when issues of conflicting values arise.[21] Although this is true, ultimately it is the behavior of individuals that produces an organization's ethical landscape—its ethical climate. Individuals acquire the proper and acceptable way of behaving in the organization through socialization. They learn the values that are operative and rewarded, which then creates the business ethical adaptedness.[22]

The 7 modern sins:
Politics without principles
Pleasures without conscience
Wealth without work
Knowledge without character
Industry without morality
Science without humanity
Worship without sacrifice

Canon Frederick Donaldson

CHAPTER 2
DRAWING THE SKIRMISH LINE

The real problem is in the hearts and minds of men. It is not a problem of physics but of ethics. It is easier to denature plutonium than to denature the evil from the spirit of man.

Albert Einstein

We live in a fanatically driven universe, characterized by rapid technological breakthroughs and high-speed dissemination of information. Our culture is primarily fixated on a self-gratification mentality that is lacking foundational, absolute principles that deal with truth and right and wrong. Feasting on this trendy, "little god" attitude, society has kicked foundational absolutes to the back of the bus only to replace them with relative ambiguity. In essence, ethical standards and morality are relative; self-determination is based on I-ism. Unfortunately, this "law of self-preservation," or "me first," attitude is not self-contained. It spills over into all aspects of society— particularly the business community, which is the bedrock of America's economic force.

Having robustly presented an opinionated position, the challenge becomes validation. In essence, is there clear evidence substantiating that prized foundational truths have given way to the realm of relativity? If so, does this hinder the business community in achieving its overall objective of creating wealth for its owners? First we must accept the assertion that the business community consists of a multitude of stakeholders representing both individuals and organizations. Then the unsolved question becomes, is there a connection between individual ethical astuteness and corporate ethical adaptableness driven by relativity and the firm's ability to continuously sustain its performance?

In the quest for resolving, or even understanding, the dilemma, researchers over the years have considered a multitude of variables and sample populations. Fortune 500 companies have been a prime population target. In one study, researchers sought to isolate a set(s) of factors predictive of corporate misconduct. After extensive analysis they theorized that with the exception of manufacturing violations, the measures of firm and industry characteristics were not strong predictors of corporate illegality. Nevertheless, the study did reveal that firm size, industry mean firm size, and industry mean asset per employee were significant indicators of total (non-minor) court proceeding violations.[23]

Using this same, well-liked population sample, Cochran and Nigh examined the relationship between the probability of a company being a non-minor violator and various firm characteristics. They discovered that a number of characteristics increased the likelihood of illegal undertaking; namely poor profitability performance, the size of the firm, magnitude of product diversification, and rapid growth.[24]

Yet in another corporate illegality study employing the same population base—that is, Fortune 500 companies—Baucus and Near found that poor-performing firms were not prone to commit wrongdoings. The researchers developed an illegal corporate behavior model using event history and identifiable illegal acts that managers and the firm knew, or should have known, were ethically questionable acts. Their findings suggest that (a) large firms that operate in dynamic, munificent environments were the most likely to behave illegally; (b) firms having a history of prior violations increase their probability of behaving illegally; and (c) firms belonging to certain industries have an increased likelihood of engaging in illegal activities.[25]

Despite the overwhelming evidence of corporate wrongdoing, relevant research is fragmented. Scholars McKendall and Wagner departed from previously established norms by focusing on violations of environmental regulations as opposed to antitrust violations, which are commonly employed in corporate-illegality research. They discovered that lower profitability is associated with higher frequencies of detected serious violations of federal environmental laws. Size, structural complexity, decentralization, and ethical climate are also associated with detected instances of serious environmental violations.[26]

Regrettably, the general public does not know the full extent of business illegality, but available evidence suggests that a significant number of large manufacturing firms routinely violate federal laws. Clinard, Yeager, Brisette, Petraskek, and Harries (1979) reported that, of the 582 largest publicly owned corporations during 1975 and 1976, manufacturing firms incurred an average of 4.8 percent enforcement actions during the observation phase and that 40 percent engaged in repeated violations.[27] A similar finding was reported by Thornburg (1991), which revealed that between 1970 and 1980, 20 percent of the sampled Fortune 500 companies had been convicted or penalized for serious violations.[28]

Evidence from these and other studies demonstrates the idea that relationships between antecedent conditions that include financial performance, industry performance, environmental factors, market consumer relations, and illegal behavior are more complex than previous theories have suggested.[29] The dilemma is further hampered because relevant research continues to be splintered and spans a variety of disciplines, which includes law in addition to the social and behavioral sciences. Furthermore the few quantitative studies that attempt to link unethical behavior and firm performance pertain almost exclusively to antitrust violations.[30] Essentially, antitrust violations are the standard for qualifying as well as quantifying unethical behavior or illegality—a tremendous limiting factor.

I must admit that the topic of unethical behavior in the business community piqued my interest many years ago as I began to detect blatant unethical practices, such as embezzlement and fraudulent reporting, gaining a foothold in many firms. As a member of the corporate world, and having achieved a fair amount of promotions along with experiencing a growing connection with the corporate "family," I began to brood over the possibility of a connection between unethical behavior and a firm's propensity for effective sustainable performance. Most assuredly, with this seemingly ageless nagging thorn, my doctoral dissertation topic focused on understanding the relationship between unethical behavior and firm performance effectiveness. Completely unaware of the magnitude of my self-gratifying endeavor, I set out to solve the great mystery—understanding if there was any glue between unethical behavior and a firm's performance effectiveness. And if so, how much?

In a desire to further understand, or even clarify, this phenomenon, I explored the topic of the relationship between individual and organizational unethical behavior and organizational performance effectiveness. Since I have a great propensity to be all encompassing, even wordy, for once I decided to really listen to the voice of experts—contain your study. So doing, I presumed several limitations: one, based on my understanding of the many faces of ethics, I restricted ethical behavior to the concept of moral development—that is, moral reasoning. This concept combines moral philosophy and cognitive psychology.[31] Embracing this lone definition, my study did not delve into the many highly recognized concepts and theories presented in the ethics and morality literature. Moreover, being fully cognitive of the broad span of literature dealing with ethics and morality, I chose to only explore business ethics and its ramifications in the corporate environment. Lastly, I did not engage in assessing corporate social responsibility, which is a valid but extremely vague concept that is ill-defined and enormously difficult to measure.[32]

With this defensible background, I restricted my search to understanding the complexity of firm performance effectiveness and ethical behavior to two hypotheses.

1. There are no relationships between perceived organizational ethical behavior and organizational performance effectiveness according to the traditional financial performance measures (return of sales, return on equity, and return on assets). The independent variable was perceived organizational ethical behavior while the financial performance measures served as the dependent variable.

2. There is no relationship between perceived individual ethical behavior and organizational performance according to the traditional financial performance measures (return on sales, return on equity, and return on assets). The independent variable was perceived individual ethical behavior while the financial performance measures served as the dependent variable.

Overly confident, and armed with an inspiring precedent background, I forged ahead, feverishly determined to expose the relationship between ethical behavior and organizational effectiveness. After all, I wanted desperately to support my own biased, yet untested, opinion. Moving swiftly down naivety lane, I immediately faced the first of many hurdles—how can a cultural, religious, and philosophical concept such as ethical behavior be precisely measured? To my consternation, there was no single acceptable device that could capture the essence of ethical behavior (remember, in many previous studies antitrust violations were primarily used to capture unethical/illegal behavior). But after extensive digging, accompanied by immense aggravation, two highly acclaimed theories, which each have their own reliable measuring instrument, surfaced: moral reasoning and ethical climate types.

Moral reasoning encases the rules and standards for what individuals should do, i.e., the ability to discern right from wrong and to reason ethically about issues.[33] Based on this concept, an instrument known as The Defining Issues Test was developed. The multi-choice test, consisting of twelve questions in each of the six dilemmas, captures individual ethical behavior.[34] The participant is required to read and select how they would respond to each, and then rank the four most important. The statements are constructed to represent various stages of moral reasoning.

In order to gauge organizational ethical behavior, Victor and Cullen's Ethical Climate Questionnaire was used. The Ethical Climate Types theory espouses the notion that organizations have a multiplicity of work climates that influence situations, the type of ethical conflict considered, and the process undertaken to solve the conflict.[35] The questionnaire is designed to accomplish two tasks: one, record the respondent's perception regarding how organizations normally make decisions involving events, practices, and procedures that mandate ethical criteria. Secondly, the questionnaire aims to identify the firm's decision-making norms with direct links to supporting forms

cal behavior might have a negative impact on a firm's ability to achieve sustained profitability. Studies over the years have shown both positive and negative relationships, as well as no relationship. Therefore, no conclusive concrete evidence has surfaced to fully support the premise that successful firms are ethical firms.

Therefore, without supporting evidence, does it really matter how companies operate? Should firms continue to view the world through eyes diagnosed as having cataracts—that is, overflowing with unethical behavior—or should firms undergo cataract surgery to remove all traces of unethical behavior? Although the choice is open for debate, the dominant underpinning exposes an overwhelming burden for the sustainability of the American business community and its negative influence on the citizenry.

Similar to Nehemiah (1:5-7), who was greatly disturbed over the condition of the wall protecting Jerusalem, I am deeply saddened over America's gradual rejection of the fundamental, godly principles that once formed our protective wall. But there is hope! Just as Jerusalem's protective wall was rebuilt in fifty-two days, our distinguished American business community can be restored to a place of incomparable dominance, surpassing all expectations.

CHAPTER 3
STAGGERING BLINDFOLDED

The quest for riches darkens the sense of right and wrong.

Antiphanes

As a nature lover, I fully enjoy and receive great pleasure in seeing a beautifully landscaped garden—a plot of land overflowing with carefully selected plants, trees, and other ornaments. What a great joy! Then again, if this great stunning masterpiece is left to itself, thistles and thorns eventually will completely overshadow the once-cherished beauty. To remain a center of enjoyment, the garden has to be nurtured; to be precise, it has to be watered, pruned, and fed. Likewise, uncontrolled unethical behavior, left to itself, feeds on itself and escalates beyond any resemblance to ethical and moral aptitude.

According to historians, America has been at this regrettable crossroads three different times. Each time the general public took a stand and was unwilling to tolerate rampant unethical behavior—they demanded action.[42]

The first uproar, occurring between the late 1800s to World War I, resulted in the development of the Sherman and Clayton Antitrust Acts, the Federal Reserve System, the Federal

Trade Commission, and regulations regarding food and drugs. The second time the public's trust was betrayed was during the depression era in the 1930s. The huge losses many Americans suffered resulted in major outcry targeted at the business world. Numerous institutions were established, namely the Federal Deposit Insurance Corporation, the National Labor Relations Board, and others that oversaw different aspects of business operations. The third period, beginning in the 1960s and peaking between 1973 and 1980, fostered an emphasis on corporate social responsibility and protection for the consumer.[43]

Now the question is, have we entered the fourth slump of unchecked unethical behavior? Have the citizens of this great country reached a point of intolerance? Gauging from the recent thermometer readings, we have an increasingly distressed, frustrated, and suspicious general public. If public opinion polls represent reliable indicators, the results support the premise that America has indeed reached this fourth period.

The reins of self-control are gone. Polls taken by the *New York Times, U. S. News and World Report,* and *Time* magazine disclosed a troublesome climate. These polls testify that 55 percent of the American public believes corporate executives are dishonest; 69 percent think that most employees steal for personal use; 60 percent believe business people overstate their expense reports; and 76 percent blame the business community for the country's decline in morality. Not surprisingly, the general public believes that the greatest threat to America is big business.[44] Whether this notion is valid or not, it is what the great citizens of America believe. We should be seriously concerned.

An attitude similar to the one exhibited in the opinion polls was evident when 1,324 workers, managers, and executives, representing various industries, participated in a survey. The participants were required to identify violations attributable to perceived job pressures, such as long hours, job security, balancing work and family, and personal debt: 48 percent admitted to unethical or illegal activities that included cheating on an expense report, paying or accepting kickbacks, secretly forging a signature, or ignoring environmental violations. While the survey reveals acceptance of unethical behavior, it unfortunately does not account for the many unreported employee-initiated violations that are attributed to perceived job pressure.[45]

According to a study conducted by the Society for Human Resource Management and the Ethics Resource Center, perceived employee job pressures and conflicts of interest, which often stem from management, play fundamental roles in dishonest activities within a company. The most commonly cited source of pressure to compromise ethical standards was following the boss's directive.[46] Similarly, 48 percent and 40 percent of the respondents, respectively, stated that meeting overly aggressive business objectives and reacting to the firm's survivor tactics exerted pressure to compromise one's ethical standards.[47] Comparable results were reported by a KPMG study, which discovered that 76 percent of employees engaged in illegal or unethical conduct at work, 45 percent admitted lying to a superior within the prior year, and 36 percent lied or falsified a written report.[48]

To combat the unprecedented proliferation of unethical behavior, the business community, besides attempting to police itself, has endured an abundance of regulations, such as Congressional Sentencing Guidelines and the Sarbanes-Oxley Act, which are designed to restrain unethical corporate behavior. Even with these well-intended actions, the flaunting of ethical defiance on the part of the business community constantly bombards us. Perhaps accountability is ill-focused? Instead of focusing entirely on corrective actions applicable to the business realm, dare we explore the constituents, i.e., the individuals? Arriving at the same assertion, Arnott theorized that the realms of business and politics are merely a reflection of society.[49] Therefore, before positive results can be acknowledged in the business community, societal ethics has to improve. When taking this position, we are forced to address several questions—how pervasive is societal corruption, and when does corruptive behavior kickoff?

Evidence points to (a) an early beginning of corruptive behavior and (b) an infusion at all levels of society, regardless of gender, ethnicity, education, or economics. For example, according to a Josephson Institute study, 40 percent of elementary students admitted stealing something they wanted within the past year, even if it meant stealing from a friend. Also noted in the study, 40 percent of the young men and 30 percent of the young women participated in shoplifting.[50] This dishonorable behavior trend was also observable at the university level. Based on results from a Rutgers University study, 70 percent of students admitted to cheating on an exam in the past year while 87 percent cheated on assignments. In order to improve their chance of being accepted into graduate school, 60 percent of graduate students say they cheated. This percentage increased to 75 percent for MBA students.[51]

Not a pretty picture. Our society is infused with unrepentant corruptive deeds. Thistles and thorns abound! Unattended and loosely upheld by many in our society, unethical behavior now flourishes—in our schools, government, businesses, and lives. Since there is an inherent, debatable difficulty with measuring ethical rightness, the general public and the business community might be ill-informed about the severity of either the moral quandary or the possible negative effects unscrupulous deeds have on firm performance effectiveness—which impacts the cost of products and the firm's ability to enhance shareholder value.

Although we are saturated with media coverage about the recent, and seemingly unprecedented, proliferation of unethical behavior in the business environment, this is a problem that has existed for eons. As reported earlier, its impact has resulted in a steady decline of the public's confidence in American businesses, which appear to breed and stomach the kind of unscrupulous behavior that costs firms billions annually.[52] Be reminded that the general public customarily absorbs the consequences of corruptive practices through higher consumer prices. This is no surprise. Businesses habitually adhere to a pass-through theory. The cost of the illegality becomes a cost of doing business, the same as buying equipment, paying employees, and acquiring insurance. If not passed on to the consumer, who would absorb the cost? To them, it isn't really a choice: either the consumer or the firm's profits will suffer.

Now here is the dilemma. Since the precise cost of these practices escapes the notice of the general public—because they remain mysterious—public outcry is minimal. In reality, the general public—the consumer—should be outraged and demand accountability from the business community regarding the cost of unethical behavior. As a group consumers are paying for wrongful acts committed by others either for personal gain or the betterment of the firm, which historically has been fixated on the bottom line and not creating shareholder's wealth.

Sadly, the history of American firms has been to measure performance success from a bottom-line perspective with a short-term fixation. Having this short-term mentality, executives emit signals that promote the idea that profitability and financial performance are more important than other objectives, such as achieving superb quality and being a good environmental steward.[53] With this mindset, the business culture shows apathy toward rules that previously guided enterprises. The prevailing attitude emerging today is one that sanctions "anything goes" as long as the firm's financial objectives are achieved. Consequently, individuals engage in fudging a few sales numbers, shortchanging customers, writing deceptive internal reports, outright lying, or even telling the boss what is desired rather than what is the truth. These actions often occur when individuals fear for their jobs if targeted financial objectives do not materialize.[54]

When job-loss threats, the misuse of corporate funds, or other corrupt activities remain anonymous or are considered acceptable practices, the organization suffers in the short-term. Nevertheless the most significant adverse effects manifest themselves in the long-term, because successful companies operate on a foundational network of dependency built on trust that binds managers, employees, shareholders, lenders, suppliers, and customers.[55] This dependency is as fundamental as the human skin's ability to regenerate and function.

The human skin is the body's largest organ and regenerates constantly. It renews itself every three to five weeks while shedding billions of skin cells daily. This steady regeneration is necessary because the skin is the body's first line of defense against infections, dehydration, and injuries. In addition, the skin serves to prevent infectious germs from entering into the body's circulatory system. This relationship between regeneration and functionality, unless bombarded by trouble, most often is treated with apathy.[56] Apathy cannot wipe away anything! It is not an eraser. Instead, the indifference breeds unhealthiness. This principle is observable not only in skincare but also in fraudulent business transactions. Rather than ignoring the beast, the business community needs to understand it and its potential relationship with long-term organizational performance effectiveness. In other words, instead of covering over or ignoring the reality of corruption within its walls, why not face the grim reality of the state of affairs? There is much to be gained. Critics advocate that applying ethics in the business community generates societal benefits that spread through the firm, its employees, and their clients.[57] In essence, shedding apathetic and unprincipled mentality in the business community has the propensity to greatly strengthen the tapestry of society.

If America embraces this challenge and takes action, any semblance of apathy must be weeded out and replaced with a mindset of constant regeneration. Dead cells (corruption) must be shed and vibrant cells (integrity) built to ward off unhealthy attacks. This will ultimately lead to economically strong and sustainable business wellness, which will in turn lead to increased wealth for shareholders.

Putting aside, if one can, the financial estimation associated with wrongful acts, other costs, such as the latent deterioration in societal morality, have to be considered. The societal effect fosters distrust between providers, the business entity, and the consumer. This is partly due to the popular perception that the penalties for illegal business behavior are too lenient. This perceived inequity, so widely held by many and supported by the outcome of many of the notorious scandals that have occurred in the last decade, potentially places the American economic system at risk. In general most Americans not only see inequities in application but also concede that corruption is bad for America.[58]

Just how bad? A. Huffington puts forth a good argument in her book, *Pigs at the Trough: How Greed and Political Corruption are Undermining America*. She asserted that many corporate executives actively engaged in abusive and unethical behavior that drove them to falsely depict the firm's financial wellness. On a personal basis, they gained substantial wealth while the organization under their guidance performed poorly. These abusive executives—aided by a cast of enablers, such as investment analysts, accountants, and corporate board members—successfully hinder needed financial reform in the business sector through lobby initiatives and political maneuvering. At the end of the day these caretakers fail to acknowledge their paramount responsibility—creating wealth for the owners. Instead, the owners of the enterprises, the investors, absorb the unpleasant effects of the appalling behavior.[59]

When unprincipled business tactics are pursued, the short-term performance conceivably might be attractive, but the long-term impact has the capacity to be devastating. For example the Chrysler Corporation, acting unethically, purposely disconnected odometers and later reconnected them in order to sell the automobiles as new. As a result, they faced fines up to $120 million. Clearly Chrysler's questionable actions affected the firm's performance effectiveness.[60] In a similar manner, Prudential Insurance suffered a $35 million fine for the use of deceptive sales practices and settled a class action suit valued at nearly $410 million which granted restitution to policyholders.[61]

Without a doubt, dishonest behavior is costly. It reduces government tax receipts, increases the price of products, increases the cost to adhere to additional legislation, and ultimately it has the potential to place a company's long-term profitability at risk despite the possibility that there might be short-term attractiveness.[62] In essence, when the firm or its employees insistently satisfy the craving of the eyes, the yearning of the flesh, and the narcissism of life, sorrow looms. Damaged creditability, weakened shareholder value, and potential bankruptcy abound. This is a dreadful price to pay for meeting the analyst's quarterly projection! Or being the highest paid CEO; avoiding environmental regulations; knowingly selling defective products; falsifying financial records; saving money by hiring undocumented workers; or employing off-book practices by using cash.

I am absolutely convinced that no wealth in the world can help humanity forward...Money only appeals to selfishness and always irresistibly tempts its owner to abuse it. Can anyone imagine Moses, Jesus or Gandhi with the moneybags of Carnegie?

Albert Einstein.

CHAPTER 4
BRINGING BACK THE ARK

To accomplish great things, we must dream as well as act.

Anatole France

In our fast-paced society, which is characterized by a microwave mentality, while problems are easily pointed out, finding real solutions for them seldom happens or is even desired. Students of yesteryear understood that presenting a problem is simply not enough, regardless of how well the problem is packaged. In order to derive meaningful solutions they discovered that there was a great need to understand not only the cause but also the effect. Without this process, the intrinsic value of the problem is questionable. Applying this same principle, I admit that merely assembling and rendering the problem of unethical behavior in the business community has no value without considering the underlying element—the impact to the enterprise.

Any unethical behavior incident occurring within the enterprise has an associated cost. These costs might include, but are not limited to, high susceptibility to revenue loss, the squandering or misuse of valuable resources, lawsuits spawned by questionable integrity, unsatisfied customers, investor aban-donment, and significant employee flight. Therefore, by pro-actively engaging in establishing a solid ethical foundation, the firm seizes the opportunity to minimize exposure. Even though research findings are inconclusive, many practitioners, includ-ing myself, contend that establishing an ethical base plays a decisive factor in a firm's sustainability. This foundation is es-sential if American business leaders, the caretakers of the na-tion' enterprises, want to maintain world-class leadership. They must seriously demonstrate a strong sense of ethical and moral values if they hope to ward off the growing trend, which shows that the younger generation is extremely sanguine about cheat-ing. After all, many of these individuals who appear to have little if any reservations about immoral behavior are our future business leaders.[63]

Regrettably, unlike many fashion trends that absorb society for a short duration, the immoral scandals mesmerizing much of today's media coverage are not just today's problems; they are like a forest fire burning out of control. Unless there is a concerted effort and a willingness on the part of the business community to douse the flame of corruption, it will continue to burn. Feeding on itself, the blaze epitomized by immoral behaviors such as lusting after fleshly things (absorbed with amassing self-gratifying wealth at the expense of others), lust-ing with the eyes (absorbed with, I see, I want, it is mine), and pure egotistical pride (absorbed by self with little regard for others) will consume our great nation.

Yes! We have a noble nation that surpasses all others in natural beauty—a pleasure my husband and I often explore. When travel becomes part of our busy agenda, planning is an essential and elementary component because the designated route shapes the total mileage, driving time, hotels, restau-rant, rest areas, and probable costs. Without thinking or even verbalizing, we are applying a simple principle played out in every management course—to achieve a desired destination (end result) one needs a road map delineating direction, necessary amenities, and cost. This same basic principle is applicable when a firm wishes to alter its direction. The transition compels rethinking, retooling, and reevaluating how the business will be managed. What route will be taken? What are the necessities? What is the cost to stay on the downward, unethical slope (the long-term effects to the firm) or to venture to remove the cancerous beast?

Hopefully by indulging in my passionate desire to rekindle the business community's ethical and moral appetite, you are boldly prompted to step outside the proverbial box, catch the vision, and consider five common-sense principles I contend will make a significant difference in any organization. Just as a medical prescription rightly warns the patient, be aware a successful transition calls for a complete transformation—not just re-routing the unethical slope but also eliminating it. It mandates shedding the microwave mentality with its quest for immediate gratifications centered on beating the analyst's target or quarterly thinking. Instead, the transition brings about a mindset infused with a pledge, persistence, and perseverance—a pledge to change, persistence in the change, and perseverance during the change. Are you ready for the ride? The rewards are unimaginable.

The way to succeed is never quit. That's it. But really be humble about it.

Alex Haley

> *Nearly all men can stand adversity, but if you want to test a man's character, give him power.*

Abraham Lincoln

PRINCIPLE 1

An organization's ethical standard mirrors the head not the tail.

KEY DISCOVERY POINTS

- Unearthing the order
- Gauging the order

Food for thought! Have you ever watched a dog chase his or her own tail? Interestingly, no matter how hard or long the chase, the feat is never accomplished. Eventually we observe a very frustrated dog moving on to other "dog" activities. It is completely unaware of its canine physical construct, which prohibits the head and tail from making the direct contact. Many times when organizations attempt to be ethically compliant, they will mimic a canine—that is, chase with remarkable effort, yet experience little or no results. Why? Mostly because they're deficient in understanding an organization's construct—the ageless design chasm!

Since the beginning of time scholars and practitioners have been talking about the leader vis-à-vis leadership. Annals spanning over thousand of years reflect many deeds and contributions of well-know leaders: Moses leading the children of Israel out of slavery into the promised land; Jesus Christ introducing concepts and teachings about love and forgiveness that were revolutionary; George Washington leading a brand-new nation into battle and demonstrating that the Declaration of Independence, which had been signed the previous year, was far more than simply an idealistic dream; and Abraham Lincoln, daring to declare freedom for the oppressed slaves.

Although there has been an immense interest in leadership throughout history and even today, serious studies on the subject matter did not commence until the 1920s.[64] Evidence of this proliferation is seen in the many volumes of books and articles attempting to not only delineate skills and styles that will ensure effective leadership, but also what constitutes leadership. While there is extensive research as well as an unmanageable volume of self-help manuals describing the necessary skills and competencies of effective leaders, there is little scholarly exploration into the inner character of the leader. This is particularly troublesome since leadership ultimately comes down to a question of character—to be precise, the complex and ethical traits which distinguish one individual from another individual. No one person is the same.

Using an old management adage about peeling the onion to arrive at the foundational truth, we see that character can best be described as having three dimensions: personality, values, and spirituality. The first dimension, personality, reflects how one relates to others and to self. Secondly, values are an indication of one's inner belief system concerning modes of behavior. Finally, one's spirituality determines the inner-meaning system that makes sense of life. Taken in totality, all three dimensions interact to influence the perceptions and behaviors of the leader. Accordingly, the leader's character is extremely relevant and important to the organization; it influences the entire organization. It is the adhesive between organizational trust, organizational culture, and organizational longevity. Aside from being the great influencing factor within the firm, the leader's character is firmly linked with the leader's credibility.[65]

Picture Niagara Falls: Majestic! Beautiful! Water, swiftly cascading with purpose, generating energy. That should be the leader's credibility—surging with energy throughout the ranks as members perceive the leader's ethical actions. Learning the old-fashioned way—that is, through hard experience—a good perception is not granted automatically by one's position, but instead it has to be earned. In my younger management days, full of self-importance and knowing everything, I quickly learned a valuable lesson: Authority is earned! Feeling full of gusto and swimming in pride, I proudly issued a command to a group of seasoned employees. Need I tell you the results? They laughed as I exited the room. Too crushed to go back into their office, I resolved to wait to see what would happen. Nothing! They simply ignored my directives. It was a painful lesson but one never forgotten—leaders must be about earning. There are no giveaways! Accordingly, to be perceived as an ethical leader, members of the organization have to see the leader as being both a moral person and a moral leader. The moral person's foundation is grounded in his or her traits, behavior, and decisions. Of all the known traits, integrity is the one most often associated with a leader. It is regarded as being a holistic attribute that includes both honesty and trustworthiness.[66]

The leader, besides being perceived as honest and trustworthy, is charged with developing a reputation for ethical leadership, not just with key employees but all employees. In other words, the leader must make ethics and values a salient aspect of the leadership agenda. Not easy! Most likely it requires bold action akin to a situation I experienced in the eighties. Personal computers were beginning to position themselves as vital components in day-to-day business operations, yet a number of us treated the smart-box as an office decoration or a status symbol. Without warning, the company's president boldly announced, "Use your e-mail for all communication between your peers and me; refrain from written memorandum or calls unless absolutely necessary." Wow! What a change! Within weeks we experienced an overwhelming improvement in office communications. He had great foresight; he surmised the technological trend and its pending impact on conducting business in the future. He knew adaptation was critical; it would enable the firm to continue to effectively operate with the changing times. The president made it a salient part of his agenda.

For the leader, to make ethics and morality a vital part of the agenda is not easy, particularly when the traditional business landscape is riddled with messages about beating the competition and achieving or bettering quarterly goals and profits. However, through personal actions the leader has to time after time communicate ethical values commensurate with being the Chief Ethics Officer.

This suggests that ethical leadership implies the person is well-grounded in a set of values and beliefs that would be viewed as being ethical. One could describe the leader as being a typical house painter: selecting the color tones, purchasing the paint, securing the correct paintbrushes, and controlling the painting process. During the painting transition, all members of the household have to endure the process—that is, the odor, misplaced furniture, picture-free walls, etc. Yet on completion everyone enjoys the makeover. Similarly, ethical leadership touches more than the leader. It can be equated to an artist painstakingly crafting a handmade quilt. The construction process is time-consuming, but once completed it emits joy, pride, and warmth to the user. Ethical leadership, like the quilt, literally envelops the entire organization, resulting in a proud, committed, and loyal workforce.[67]

The framework of an organization, for practical purposes, resembles the family institution. As a youngster, our family meals, particularly dinner, required full attendance—no exceptions. There were two non-negotiable musts: one, my father insisted we eat at the table together; and two, we had to eat what was prepared. My father had established guidelines regarding meals that were non-negotiable, and as such, a number of lessons were learned. The first lesson taught that non-negotiable guidelines are necessary in families as well as organizations. With only a sixth grade education, my father understood the importance of having an assembled gathering consistently. The second lesson imparted that communication is vital in any environment. Lastly, learning to eat what was put forward taught flexibility, a necessity for well-roundedness. My father led the charge with uncompromising vigor.

Similar to my father's adamant position, the leader's primary job is to see what is good for the company and employees, and then create something for the well-being of the organization.[68] This is perhaps more important today than ever because the new organizational landscape revolves around many employees working independently and off-site, with little or no direct supervision. In these new organizations, values are the glue that can hold the things together; therefore, these values must be conveyed from the top of the organization repeatedly through words and deeds.[69]

By way of the head, that is the leader, compliance to ethical behavior is by all means attainable. But certainly not with a canine mentality! To achieve the goal of being ethically compliant, the head has to lead the charge, understand the organization's design chasms, and then systematically eradicate them, armed with a self-assured character grounded in values, spiritually, and creditability.

CONSIDER

Greatness is no small matter. In leaders it mandates exhibiting profound attributes without fanfare while creating an environment of hope and betterment for society. Great leaders share a common thread—responding to their call (their passion). Like clockwork, they demonstrate a self-assured character grounded in spiritually and values that render them as trustworthy and honest. Since they are not self-focused, which can breed insecurity, they consistently surround themselves with persons expert in areas they are lacking. Without reservations, they admit ignorance in some areas and understand that no one individual knows everything. A teenager might not agree with this assessment, but age and experience will support my position.

An outstanding leader once told me, "Don't let your ego prevent you from achieving. Strategically surround yourself with knowledgeable persons equipped to fill your know-how void."

GREAT LEADERS

- Winston Churchill
- Nelson Mandela
- Mahatma Gandhi
- Martin Luther King Jr.
- Billy Graham

We don't accomplish anything in this world alone…and whatever happens is the result of the whole tapestry of one's life and all the weavings of individual threads from one to another that creates something.

Sandra Day O'Connor

PRINCIPLE 2

The organization is one body with many members.

KEY DISCOVERY POINTS

- Accepting organizational oneness purely as a oneness
- Capitalizing on the power of the oneness.

When most of us think about organizations, our minds immediately turn to corporations. Nevertheless there are other forms: the sole propriety and partnerships. At the very heart of each form is the concept of "body." The term "body" more often than not conjures up images of a well-toned physical structure with limitless capabilities. Yet we see another glimpse of "body" when Paul the Apostle ably tells the Corinthians, "the body is one, and has many members, and all the members of that one body, being many, are one body, so also in Christ" (1 Corinthians 12:12). He skillfully uses the physical body to demonstrate this biblical truth. Guess what, folks? The eye or ear working independently will not perform as a body. However when all of the diverse body parts collectively work together, they can actually achieve stated purposes, such as driving a car, running in a triathlon, delivering a speech, eating a healthy meal, or contemplating a difficult situation.

This same truth (principle) applies to organizations. It is a body made up of many members—individuals of diverse backgrounds, cultures, experiences, and aspirations. If we understand the acceptable business model to be symbolized by the belief that an organization is made up of individuals, that there is an intrinsic value in diversity, and that the capitalist system is built on contractual relationships, it becomes clear that the organization's focus has to begin with a concept of persons. This is an inclusive perspective that includes as many people as necessary to achieve the stated organizational purpose. Achieving the stated purpose far outweighs many prejudices, such as physical ability, race, and religion. It is long-term focused and properly places meeting the quarterly targets or annual bonuses in their rightful place; these are events and not decision-makers. They are not "concept of persons" qualifiers.

According to Max Depree, embracing the concept of persons demands that the purpose-driven organization creates an environment that recognizes certain basic fundamentals.[70] For the employee this includes being needed, cared about, and involved in the action. Being given the opportunity to do ones best and receiving fair wages and benefits is important to all the members of the organization. The environment should also be one that encourages as well as facilitates the ability to reach ones full potential. When considering these basics, does it remind you of a famous saying? "So in everything do to others what you would have them do to you" (Matthew 7:12). Truly not a bad idea!

Moreover, creating a milieu where the members of the organization are inspired to be faithful, take risks, and learn together further lends itself to the concept of persons: valuing the individual's personhood, building individual value, and contributing selflessly. When practiced, the concept of persons yields an increase in the sum total of the organization. Not only does the individual profit by the development, but also, without a doubt, the organization will experience enormous benefit. In my younger career days, when companies overtly demonstrated that they truly valued their workers, your peers considered you a traitor if you voiced any negative thoughts about your employer. Today, according to many studies and surveys, most individuals dislike their jobs, have little or no admiration for their employers, and don't trust them. This is a problem! An even graver problem considering that we now operate in a global economy.

In this ever-changing global marketplace, due to the sheer diversity of the employee base, applying the concept of persons, which adds value by building a cadre of dedicated and faithful members, becomes more critical. Unlike the traditional domestic US marketplace prior to the 1980s, the international setting (the national cultural or national character) becomes extremely important for a number of reasons. First, inhabitants of a particular country share a national moral fiber that is more apparent to foreigners than to the nationals themselves. Secondly, since culture is a collective mental programming, change is very difficult; and, if change occurs, the process is extremely slow because the condition is shared among all inhabitants. Their common belief, stemming from the common culture, is crystallized in all institutions—the family structure, religious organizations, forms of government, and law literature.[71]

The common beliefs, which are at the heart of the national culture or characteristic, dictate values, perceptions, and interpretations. Examples are readily found in acceptable or non-acceptable food, work attire, and even in the recognition of religious holidays. Therefore, in applying the much-desired person inclusiveness, the organization has to understand or be cognitive of national values, perceptions, and interpretations. Several years ago during a brief stay in Africa, I committed and unforgivable act, although I knew better. I used my left hand to greet a tribal chief. A definite no-no! My obvious lack of appreciation for national culture resulted in my insulting a very important member of the host team. I potentially damaged a relationship.

When taking into account the changing economic horizon, functional mandates of the twentieth century might be ill-fit for the global marketplace of the twenty-first century. Perhaps to properly become an inclusive persons organization the time has come to remove the stigma historically associated with the Human Resource Department. This department is known for moving individuals in and out of the organization, dispensing what are usually less than desirable annual increases, and offering workshops based on some predetermined relationship. This function, traditionally, has not been properly equipped to capitalize on the firm's most valuable resource—its employees. For most organizations employee cost (that is, wages plus any benefits) accounts for the greater part of the outlay of funds.

If this is the reality, why not have the same intense focus on employees as placed on other assets? When spending funds relating to capital investments, the firm carefully considers the incremental cash flow and the resulting measurements, such as the payback period, Internal Rate of Return, and the Net Present Value. These measurements dictate acceptance or rejection of the potential investment.

Unlike creating a relevant incremental cash flow to properly gauge an investment project, many well-meaning measurements developed decades ago when cultural differences were a non-issue, are still vital parts of the Human Resource portfolio. For example, setting and measuring individual objectives as opposed to unit goals, cataloging individuals by job titles or functions and layered organizational forms, which of themselves prohibit information sharing. Many of these previously held "pillars" are potentially contra to creating an all-inclusive organization.

If then to create an all-inclusive persons organization, why not consider Asset Development or even Resource Deployment? After all, the all-inclusive persons agenda strives and encourages members to add value to the organization; it provides the opportunity for members to reach their potential; and it requires members to be faithfully committed to building wealth for shareholders. The all-inclusive persons organization is bigger than just hiring and firing employees: it is the driver in creating organizational wealth.

CONSIDER

The all-inclusive persons concept implies an organizational oneness where all persons share in a common goal—to continually build wealth for the owners. To accomplish this overriding goal, "the body" effectively communicates, shares information, develops, and reaches individual potentials, which requires members to be faithfully committed.

"ONE BODY" KILLERS

MANAGEMENT

- Executives earning wages that are truly excessive
- Massive organizational downsizing married to swelling outsourcing
- Decisions in direct conflict with cultural and religious beliefs
- Abuse of power
- Shoot the messenger mentality
- Stifle individuals as well as information

EMPLOYEES

- Diminished work ethics
- Non-committal attitude
- Hoarding information for selfish gain
- Misuse and abuse of organizational assets

Character is like a tree and reputation like its shadow. The shadow is what we think of it; the tree is the real thing.

Abraham Lincoln

PRINCIPLE 3

Ethical policies and procedures are guidance tools, not personal transformation tools.

KEY DISCOVERY POINTS

- Scoping policies and procedures
- Ranking policies and procedures

I had the glorious opportunity to work for a number of excellent companies during my corporate career days. One company in particular was inundated with policies and procedures—there were policies and procedures to explain policies and procedures. Every possible topic appeared to have been dissected and carefully documented. Besides my initial reaction of total disbelief, I am not sure whether I was impressed or overwhelmed. Nonetheless I soon realized that, although the mountainous paper bureaucracy was well-known in the organization, few understood or actually adhered to the yoke. Sadly, perhaps in this organization the unspoken motive supporting the policies and procedures was "to standardize management decision-making." Absurd! In another organization the fun began when you wanted to replace an outdated policy. Finding the policy manual was the challenge of the day. I will let you decide the importance of the policies so well documented in that eternal manual.

Policies and procedures are admirable and by all means necessary. They provide safeguards to guarantee that members of the organization observe the essential company standards, which support the firm's core values. The two directives that are commonly present in most organizations are a code of ethics and standard operating procedures. Their intent is to minimize unacceptable behavior by spelling out certain behaviors as intolerable. Nevertheless it is suggested that standard operating procedures are highly suspect of contributing to illegal or criminal acts by expelling or encouraging individuals to commit crimes on behalf of the company.[72] Undeniably, crimes committed for the good of the firm are expansive. They range from purposely rigging test results to meet criteria, to back-dating actual shipments to beef-up the current month's sales volume.

Issues with standard operating procedures are not just a standalone problem; there is also the famous code of ethics directive. I am always taken back when entering a firm's facility. If you have never noticed, among one of the first observable wall objects is usually the firm's code of ethics. Without a doubt its grandiose appearance is impressive, but contrary to belief it fails to minimize violations.[73] In reality there is a minimal connection between a code of ethics and corporate unethical violations.[74]

Although limited perhaps in effectiveness, both the code of ethics and standard operating procedures are helpful. They augment accomplishing sound responsibility, self-regulation, and the creation of a culture that promotes anti-criminal behavior within the organization. If they are quite limited in effectiveness, what then is the solution to this grave dilemma of increasingly distorted behavior? In response, one first has to recognize that individuals are guided by personal ethics based on beliefs and culture whenever they encounter moral dilemmas. Interestingly though, through the firm's socialization, individuals learn the values that are operative and rewarded.[75] They skillfully watch and emulate to bridge the gap: their interpretation of what is acceptable behavior within the organization. But knowing that policies and procedures are mere proclamations—that is, simple rules to be followed—then more in is required in order for the organization to have a suitable ethical environment.

The "more," without hesitation, has to be the firm's top leadership. Although as an individual the leader cannot one-on-one change an individual's ethical makeup, the change comes by implementing the means whereby ethical objectives are attained. In other words, the leader has to put actions to words. By their actions, leaders become a magnet, attracting others to operate according to the highest standard. It is the firm's leader that ultimately creates the moral and ethical climate—not the code of ethics or the firm's operating procedures.[76]

CONSIDER

Organizations in this global economy now consist of many culturally diverse individuals with varying beliefs and customs. Accordingly, acceptable ethical behavior will also be diverse. Practices normally considered immoral in our American business culture might be considered acceptable in some of these culturally diverse societies: for example, bribery, negotiation tactics, or even the use of child labor. The multinational organization's acceptable ethical makeup will, at best, be a hodge-podge if no corrective action is undertaken. Effectiveness will be cultural-limited. Long term, the firm will potentially suffer if acceptable behavior is learned through socialization, which essentially transfers behaviors from one culture to another and not by the promulgation of policies and procedures. Thus it will be imperative for the firm's overall wellness to embrace ethical astuteness through its leadership.

Great minds discuss ideas, average minds discuss events, and small minds discuss people.

Admiral Hyman G. Rickover

PRINCIPLE 4

Core values are not outside of the vision—they shape the vision.

KEY DISCOVERY POINTS

- Discovering the plumb-line
- Living the plumb-line

As previously hypothesized, the effective, ethical leader must be perceived as having an unwavering character where morals and values are unquestionable. This, too, is true for a long-term focused organization that is fanatical about creating an environment of sustainability. Having this well-established set of core values, its unfaltering character—steering the firm's activities on a day-to-day basis as well as long-term—is essential. These core values are not catchy phases but solid statements that define the organization. Who they are! What they stand for! What the organization is all about! Organizationally, how does this look? Snatching a quick glance at Collins and Porras' *Built to Last,* we get a glimpse of specific core ideologies belonging to visionary companies—that is, those long-term focused organizations identified as clock builders by the authors. For example:

Boeing
Integrity and ethical business
To "eat, breathe, and sleep the world of aeronautics"[77]

On the surface these core values appear simple without substance, but they are the underpinning that drive and establish the clock builder's purpose and reason for existence. Contrary to widespread belief, it is not profit! It goes much deeper. Just as the heart in vertebrate animals, by it rhythmic contractions, acts as a force pumping blood through out the body, the firm's core ideology is its heart. By its nature the core ideology drives the firm's rhythm and its stream of activities while safeguarding its continuation. It serves as the plumb line—shaping the firm's vision of who it is and where it is going. In other words, the core ideology acts as a strainer—steering strategy and operations. Since it shapes the firm's vision, it sifts out and rejects any business opportunities that might endanger or potentially take precedence over the firm's core values. They should be tamper-proof. Therefore those clock building, long-term focused companies intent on long-term sustainability fuel potential growth and change through their well-orchestrated core value goals, which form the foundational structure of the vision. With cult-like behavior, members of the organization view everything through its core ideological eyes. If it does not fit the vision, don't sweat it—just don't do it.[78] Acceptance will be in violation of the firm's plumb line.

With this intense focus, no wonder visionary, core-value–driven companies have performed well for shareholders over long periods of time and have attained outstanding long-term performance through institutional mechanisms that support what the authors called "clock building."[79] Historically these companies refrain from being enticed and drawn into the latest market hot button because of their vision, which is built on a set of uncompromised core values that don't change with each subsequent Chief Executive Officer. They are the rock-solid foundation of the firm, and when dismantled or grossly changed, the building will suffer greatly.

Many years ago, when the computer revolution was the hottest wave, a particular company decided they would start producing computers. Mind you, this company made the decision to enter into this highly competitive arena totally unprepared, lacking computer technological knowledge. I suspect the decision-makers saw a grand opportunity. It was! A new frontier with unseen boundaries! Nonetheless, after a brief life span of expending massive effort and money, the operation was closed. The question is—did producing computers fit, or was this organization more about time-telling (acting on a great idea, getting on the latest wave) or clock building?[80]

The concept of clock building can be viewed as creating an incalculable legacy, analogous to a treasured family name that transcends generations. The name Fred rings throughout my family history. It invokes pleasant thoughts of family dedication and a strong work ethic. Amazingly, without fanfare, significant meanings often become attached to a name, particularly when the lives of the name-holders were productive, contributory, or had a positive impact on society. This same principle is applicable in organizations where the core values are not outside the vision, but are the shapers of the vision. Astonishingly, this can be observed. The names of certain organizations often evoke pleasurable thoughts, such as quality producers, customer pleasers, consistent shareholder wealth generators, and activists for the betterment of society.

CONSIDER

The core values, or the firm's ideology, are the bedrock for the successful firm. These values most often clarify the purpose and intent of the organization through answering the questions, who we are, what we stand for, and what we are all about. Since the core values are firm-specific, any commonality among firms is random. Nevertheless at the heart of the concept of firm ideology is that it gives much-needed guidance to all of the organization's members.[81] The total organization is working on the same page—contrary to a divided house that, given time, will certainly fall.

OBSERVATIONS

1. When the "known, acceptable, and practiced" core values are completely altered by a succeeding Chief Executive Offices, organization havoc ensues and leads to an unfocused environment subject to disaster.

2. There is no "right" set of core values—it is the entrenchment of these values within the firm that counts.

3. A set of un-compromised core values enhances a firm's reputation while firms lacking a set of core values, or whose values are compromised, breed contempt.

A good reputation is more valuable than money.

Publilius Syrus

The illiterate of the 21ˢᵗ century will not be those who cannot read and write, but those who cannot learn, unlearn and relearn.

Alvin Toffler

PRINCIPLE 5

Operating under the guise of the proverbial box creates barriers and not change.

KEY DISCOVERY POINTS

- Discovering the box
- Overcoming complacency

McKenna stated that the twenty-first century would be unlike any prior period in history. It would be fraught with the rapid acceleration of technology and globalization in an environment of uncertainty.[82] When meshed together, technology, globalization, and uncertainty create an un-chartered business environment that can be terrifying to the business community. It's similar to a driver attempting to navigate traffic while talking incessantly on a cell phone and drinking hot coffee—independently any one of these chores can be extremely dangerous. Let's face it, driving can be very dangerous, since road rage appears to be the current modus operandi. Now add a chatty telephone driver who is completely oblivious to everything and everybody and you get a disastrous situation waiting to happen, particularly when the distracted driver insists on periodically taking a sip of hot coffee. The driver might be daring, but to be honest, reaching the desired destination is extremely questionable. For the driver, there is extreme risk, but it is quite definable: namely, driving, chatting while driving, and sipping hot coffee. Much like the automobile driver, the American business community is unwillingly confronting untested, twenty-first-century risk: accelerated technology, globalization, and uncertainty.

Confronting the three-legged, twenty-first century milieu is discomforting, because as a community, American firms are presented with few choices, yet they are exceedingly challenging. They must be about building firms that consistently excel in serving the shareholder's best interest both in reliability and wealth. This entails being the best at what they do and doing it with fervor, long-term. This challenge comes in the midst of a highly competitive and complex environment characterized by accelerated technology, increased globalization, and a mass-dosage of uncertainty. Accomplishing this horrendous undertaking will require firms to purposely discard previously successful, traditional tools that centered on individualism, coveted layered management, and practiced elitism. There has to be a concerted effort to move outside the comfortable proverbial box laden with complacency.

Based on my experience, before making a concerted effort to change "something" you need to understand the "something." So what are we working with? Boxes! Boxed in popular maxims! A layman such as myself would describe a box as a rectangular container with five panels and a lid: the bottom panel, the foundation, supports the four vertical side panels, which then is covered by a lid placed horizontally, creating a closed containment. Further examining the proverbial business box, we see the foundation as the firm's product-offering, which traditionally prescribes the customer base, channels of distribution, material content, and labor base. These represent the four, vertical panels that fit snuggly under the lid, the firm's leadership, which traditionally has been soaked with a hierarchical, management mentality—a mentality that is normally adverse to openness and is steeped in "this is the way we have always done it," or, "if it is not broke, don't fix it." One-way communication or a shoot the messenger attitude stifles the inflow and outflow of valuable information that will allow the firm to adapt to the changing business culture.

Without a doubt change is difficult, individually and corporately. It requires courage coupled with risk-taking. Generally speaking, society views risk as undesirable and to be avoided, even if it is inevitable. Attempting to avoid risk is so prevalent in our society that we have a massive, profitable industry serving up every imaginable type of insurance. All the same, being fully aware that the potential for loss or failure is always present, risk-taking is essential for the business community. In light of the essentiality of risk-taking, the organization, endeavoring to break down the walls of proverbial thinking has to be equipped with a leadership that is tolerant of failure. This type of leadership cultivates an environment by their words and actions to help individuals overcome their fear of failure. It further understands that failures ultimately create a culture of intelligent risk-taking that leads to the perpetual innovation necessary for an organization's sustainability. Traditional ideas grounded in personal competition (individualism) are then replaced by a culture inclined to take intelligent risk and inspire the flow of information.[83]

Besides fostering an environment that encourages intelligent risk taking, the firm shedding traditionalism abandons many ideas characteristic of the mid to latter part of the 20th twentieth century. This is absolutely necessary, because during this time the American business community had it at all: manageable competition, a thirsty domestic market, and an escalating standard of living. Also throughout this period, the American business community made great strides, excelling in many disciplines: medicine, technology, education, and production capacity. What happened? Since the later half of the twentieth century we've seen a country intoxicated by success, unable to maintain its competitive edge, and bathing in complacency. If you want a business to die, inject complacency. It is a sure killer! It implies laziness, self-satisfaction, and unawareness.

Jim Collins perhaps provides one of the best illustrations of getting beyond the killer virus—the curse of complacency. After five years of analyzing twenty-eight organizations, the driving force that he saw that enabled a mediocre, complacent firm to achieve prominence centered on the type of leadership.[84] Seems rather straightforward, but the discovery is riddled with complexity attributed to individualism and risk-taking. This type of leadership, contrary to traditional thinking demands abandoning self-glory-seeking (egoism). Through an illogical intermingling of personal humility and professional will, these leaders were highly effective in transitioning the mediocre firm.[85]

Let's look at these noteworthy, five practical principles Collins discovered.[86]

1. Creating an enduring, effective organization that consistently produces tangible results takes precedence over individualism.

2. Getting the right people, which is fundamental and comes before the "what" decisions—vision, strategy, organizational structure, and tactics.

3. Filling positions with the best people according to ability and skill.

4. Achieving sustained excellence by building a culture of self-disciplined individuals with disciplined actions that adhere to a simple principle—if it does not fit, it will not be. Period.

5. Pointing to tangible improvements, regardless of size, is powerful and builds momentum.

Losing has a pronounced effect on individuals. I recall many years ago walking through a manufacturing plant which had suffered three years of extreme poor performance. I could feel the despair. Absenteeism was high and morale low. Job performance was extremely poor, and there existed an overall apathetic mood since it was rumored the plant would eventually close. Although a plant closing was never voiced, actions by management gave the impression that the plant would close.

In contrast, winning has a motivating effect on individuals. Watch any sport event, or even sit through a spelling bee, and you will witness a contagious excitement in favor of the winners. This same holds true for a consistent core-value–driven firm. In such an establishment there is low absenteeism and high morale. The employees are excited and exhibit outstanding performance. There is an abundance of quality suggestions. People want to be part of a winning team.

CONSIDER

The proverbial box is not indestructible. Its walls can come down. Unbelievably, merely a change in the firm's mind-set is powerful. It has the power to topple walls! To Collins and my amazement, none of the successful changers are purely financial! Although mainly "soft" by nature, the key success factors are sound: the firm's leadership must be failure tolerant, not self-absorbed, place value on getting the right and best people, doing only what the company does best, and striving for tangible improvements. Destroying the traditional proverbial box filled with individualism, self-gratification, egoism, and short-term profit-taking hinges primarily on "soft" fundamentals. For the most part, measuring these "soft" fundamentals is difficult, if not impossible, yet traditional financial returns will show improved yields.

Financial yields certainly will have the tendency to improve when ratios such as the employee turnover or absenteeism rates move downward. Likewise, when the cost of quality, or pilfering, becomes a non-issue, the performance results will be startling. Stakeholders see results expressed in actions and not just words, reminiscent of what the Apostle James said, "Don't just listen to the Word of God, but do what it says. The doer of the Word will be blessed in what he does" (James 1:22).

No man will make a great leader who wants to do it all himself, or to get all the credit for doing it.

Andrew Carnegie

CHAPTER 5
LOOKING AHEAD

Success is simple. Do what is right, the right way and at the right time.

Arnold Glasow

ETHICS IN THE TWENTY-first CENTURY

The entrance of the twenty-first century was momentous—an event experienced by peoples of the entire world. But for the American business community, the historical birth arrived toting baggage filled with leftover challenges. One in particular is the troubling, unethical debacle America faces as it contemplates navigating the deep waters of unprecedented acceleration in technology, heightened competition from countries intent on being global powerhouses, and widespread uncertainty throughout the world.

As noted previously, unethical behavior is like any other virus. It continues to spread, attacking without discernment, until an antidote is discovered. Accordingly, as America moves further into the twenty-first century, one has to question the role ethics will play, particularly in areas such as the business community, technology, and institutions of learning. Each of these areas no doubt will experience increasing opportunities to engage in practices that will be ethically questionable.

In the business community, with the ever-present pressure to meet the expectations of the stockholders and to master all of the competitive forces, to what extent will businesses cave-in to appease stockholders? Will the marching orders be false financial reporting, stealing, misrepresenting critical information in quality and environmental reports? Or will we see the business community resorting more to offshore activities and/or outsourcing, via investing in countries with lower labor rates? The question them becomes, is the offshore operation only a shell? If only a shell, was its creation for the purpose of reducing taxes? Are the recipients of the outsourcing using child labor? Are they bound by environmental regulations? These acts certainly demonstrate the gnawing ethical issues for the business community.

Similarly, the acceleration in technology has created a hotbed for unethical behavior. The list of opportunities is unending: downloading proprietary music, pirating movies, copying software, and hacking of data are just a few of the dishonorable acts. Astonishingly, for many individuals, these acts do not constitute corrupt behavior. Nonetheless their actions are comparable to those actions committed by countries that habitually usurp patented technology. Technology in of itself has bred an entire coffer of ethical issues. With the growth and reliance on technology by all, ethical issues are mounting and will continue.

Ethical issues are not just limited to the business community or technology, but spill over into the medical arena and learning institutions. There is a growing movement in society that advocates euthanasia, stem cell research, and the right for individuals to have treatments withheld when faced with a terminal disease. Likewise, learning institutions are faced with students disregarding once-cherished ethical principles at an earlier age. They have no qualms about stealing and cheating. Each of these poses serious ethical issues for society.

The twenty-first century, exciting as it is, is bringing greater-than-ever opportunities for America while also delivering a mounting dilemma. What can we, or what are we going to do about the growing ethical issues? Unfortunately, with increased technology and competitive forces with varying ethical cultures, deliberate, unwarranted behavior will most likely gather speed. The consequences of this intensification bring uncertainty. Just how it will fully impact the American business community, its ability to compete in global markets, and overall camaraderie, as a nation is unknown at this time. Nevertheless, if America is to maintain its economic standing in this global world and be the guiding beacon for other powers, our ethical challenges must be harnessed. We have no choice.

A good reputation is more valuable than money.

Publilius Syrus

Notes

Chapter 1

[1] Burtness. *Morality, ethics and the future*; Thiroux. *Ethics: Theory and practice.*

[2] Bok. Henry Sigwick's Practical Ethics, 361–378.

[3] Sidgwick. Utilitarianism, 253–260.

[4] Thiroux. *Ethics: Theory and practice.*

[5] Wekesser. *Ethics.*

[6] de Spinoza. Belief in God motivates people to behave ethically, 23–31.

[7] Nietzsche. Atheism motives people to behave ethically, 23–31.

[8] Noddings. A philosophy of caring motives people to behave ethically, 38–46.

[9] Reidenbach and Robin. *Business ethics.*

[10] Halcrow. Is there a crisis in business ethics? 10–17.

[11] Brown. The academic ethics of graduate business students, 151–157.

[12] Hanson and Solomon. The real business ethics, 41.

[13] Thiroux. *Ethics: Theory and practice.*

[14] Thompson and Stickland. *Strategic Management.*

[15] Cochran and Nigh. Illegal corporate behavior and the question

of moral agent, 73–91; Fleming. A survey and critique of business ethics research.

[16] Cochran and Nigh. Illegal corporate behavior, 73–91.

[17] Cochran and Nigh. Illegal corporate behavior, 73–91.

[18] Mathews. Codes of ethics, 107–130.

[19] Frederick. *Research in corporate social performance and policy*, 1–23.

[20] Derry. Moral reasoning in work-related conflicts, 25–49.

[21] Cullen, Victor, and Stephens. An ethical weather report.

[22] Victor and Cullen. A theory and measure of ethical climate in organizations, 51–71.

CHAPTER 2

[23] Clinard, Yeager, Brisette, Petrkekk, and Harries (1979), cited in Cochran and Nigh, 1987.

[24] Cochran and Nigh. Illegal corporate behavior, 73–91.

[25] Baucus and Near. Can illegal corporate behavior be predicted? 9–36.

[26] McKendall and Wagner. Motive, opportunity, choice, and corporate illegality, 624–647.

[27] Clinard et al., study cited in McKendall and Wagner, 624–647.

[28] Thornburg study cited in McKendall and Wagner, 624–647.

[29] Baucus and Near. Can illegal corporate behavior be predicted? 9–36.

[30] McKendall and Wagner. Motive, opportunity, choice, and corporate illegality, 624–647.

[31] Kohlberg. *The philosophy of moral development*.

[32] Pava and Krausz. The paradox of social cost, 321–358.

[33] Bauer. *What is moral reasoning?*

[34] Rest. *Development in judging moral issues*.

[35] Victor and Cullen. A theory and measure of ethical climate in organizations, 51–71.

[36] Cullen, Victor, and Bronson. The ethical climate questionnaire,

667–674; Victor and Cullen. A theory and measure of ethical climate in organizations, 51–71.

[37] Agle, Mitchel, and Sonnenfeld. Who matters to CEO? 507–526; Simons, Pelled, and Smith. Making use of difference, 662–673.

[38] Wimbush. Ethical climates and ethical behavior.

[39] Baucus and Baucus. Paying the piper, 129–151.

[40] Baucus and Baucus. Paying the piper, 129–151.

[41] McKendall. Corporate governance and corporate illegality, 201–224.

CHAPTER 3

[42] Spencer. *The legal, societal, and management issues.*

[43] Spencer. *The legal, societal, and management issues.*

[44] Bowen (1987), Hoffman (1986), McLoughlin, Sheled, and Witkin (1987), Williams (1985) studies cited in Reinbach and Robin, 1989.

[45] Society. *Unethical workers and illegal acts*, 2–4.

[46] Vickers. Business ethics and the HR role, 26–31.

[47] Joseph and Esen, 2003

[48] Arnott. Ethics, earnings and equity evaluation.

[49] Arnott. Ethics, earnings and equity evaluation.

[50] Arnott. Ethics, earnings and equity evaluation.

[51] Arnott. Ethics, earnings and equity evaluation.

[52] MacLean. Thick as thieves, 167–196; McKendall. Corporate governance and corporate illegality, 624–647; Cochran and Nigh. Illegal corporate behavior, 73–91; Reidenback and Robin. *Business ethics*; Gautschi and Jones. Illegal corporate behavior and corporate board structure, 93–106; and Lipset and Schneider. *The confidence gap.*

[53] Carlisle and Carter. Fortune service and industrial 500 presidents, 77–83; Reidenback and Robin. *Business ethics.*

[54] Labich. Businesses are becoming less ethical, 110–115.

[55] Labich. Businesses are becoming less ethical, 110–115.

[56] New York-Presbysterian. Anatomy of the skin.

[57] Wekesser. *Ethics.*

[58] Gautschi and Jones. Illegal corporate behavior and corporate board structure, 93–106; Growing the Carrot, 1783–1800; Lipset and Schneider. *The confidence gap*; McKendall and Wagner. Motive, opportunity, choice, and corporate illegality, 624–647.

[59] Huffington. *Pigs at the trough.*

[60] Reidenbach and Robin. *Business ethics.*

[61] Growing the Carrot, 1783–1800.

[62] Cochran and Nigh. Illegal corporate behavior, 73–91.

Chapter 4

[63] Arnott. Ethics, earnings and equity evaluation.

[64] Goffee and Jones, 2000

[65] Judge, 2001

[66] Brown, Hartman and Trevino, 2000

[67] Brown, Hartman and Trevino, 2000

[68] Hill and Wetlaufer, 1998

[69] Brown, Hartman and Trevino, 2000

[70] DePree. *Leadership is an art.*

[71] Hofstede, 1980

[72] Cochran and Nigh. Illegal corporate behavior, 73–91.

[73] Cochran and Nigh. Illegal corporate behavior, 73–91.

[74] Matthews. Codes of ethics, 107–130.

[75] Victor and Cullen. A theory and measure of ethical climate in organizations, 51–71.

[76] Matthews. Codes of ethics, 107–130.

[77] Collins and Porras. *Built to Last*, 68–70.

[78] Collins and Porras. *Built to Last*, 68–70.

[79] Collins and Porras. *Built to Last*, 68–70.

[80] Collins and Porras. *Built to Last*, 68–70.

[81] Collins and Porras. *Built to Last*, 68–70.

[82] McKenna 2001

[83] Fason and Keyes, 2002

[84] Collins. *Good to great.*

[85] Collins. *Good to great.*

[86] Collins. *Good to great.*

REFERENCES

Agle, B., R. Mitchel, and J. Sonnenfeld. 1999. Who matters to CEO? An investigation of stakeholder attributes and salience, corporate performance and CEO values. *Academy of Management Journal* 42(5):507–526. Retrieved January 6, 2004 from ProQuest.

Arnott, R. D. 2003. Ethics, earnings and equity evaluation. *Journal of Portfolio Management* 29(3). Retrieved July 30, 2005, from EBSCOhost.

Baucus, M. S., and D. A. Baucus. 1997. Paying the piper: an empirical examination of longer-term financial consequences. *Academy of Management Journal* 40(1):129–151. Retrieved December 6, 2003, from ProQuest.

Baucus, M. S., and J. P. Near. 1991. Can illegal corporate behavior be predicted? An event history analysis. *Academy of Management Journal* 34(1):9–36. Retrieved September 4, 2003, from Business Source Premier.

Bauer, K. 2000. *What is moral reasoning?* Retrieved October 9, 2003 from University of Delaware: http://www.udel.edu. psych/kbaurer.

Bok, S. 2000. Henry Sigwick's Practical Ethics. *Utilitas* 12(3):361–378. Retrieved March 11, 2003, from Academic Search Premier.

Brown, B. 1995. The academic ethics of graduate business students: A survey. *Journal of Education for Business* 70(3):151–157. Retrieved July 2003 from Academic Search Premier.

Brown, M., Hartman, L., & Trevino, L. (2000). Moral person and moral manager: How executives develop a reputation for ethical leadership. *California Management Review, 42*(4), 128-143. Retrieved October 3, 2002, from Business Source Premier.

Burtness J. H. 1999. *Morality, ethics and the future.* Minneapolis, MN: Fortress Press.

Carlisle, A. E., and K. Carter. 1988. Fortune service and industrial 500 presidents: Priorities and perceptions. *Business Horizon* pp. 77–83. Retrieved December 1, 2003, from Business Source Premier.

Cochran, P. L., and D. Nigh. 1987. Illegal corporate behavior and the question of moral agent: An empirical examination. In W. C. Frederick, ed. *Research in corporate social performance and policy* pp. 73–91. Greenwich, CT: JAI Press.

Collins, J. 2001. *Good to great: Why some companies make the leap...and others don't.* New York: HarperCollins

Collins, J. and J. I. Porras. 1994. *Built to last: Successful habits of visionary companies.* New York: HarperCollins.

Cullen, J. B., B. Victor, and J. W. Bronson. 1993. The ethical climate questionnaire: An assessment of its development and validity. *Psychological Reports* 73:667–674.

Cullen, J. B., B. Victor, and C. Stephens. 1989. An ethical weather report: Assessing the organizations' ethical climate. *Organizational Dynamics* 18(2). Retrieved June 2003, from Business Source Premier.

DePree, M. 1989. *Leadership is an art.* New York: Dell

Derry, R. 1987. Moral reasoning in work-related conflicts. In W. C. Frederick, ed. *Research in corporate social performance and policy* pp. 25–49. Greenwich, CT: AI Press.

de Spinoza, B. 1995. Belief in God motivates people to behave ethically. In C. Wekesser, ed. *Ethics* pp. 23–31. San Diego, CA: Greenhaven Press.

Fleming, J. E. 1997. A survey and critique of business ethics research, 1986. In W.C. Frederick, ed. *Research in corporate social performance and policy pp. 1-23.* Greenwich, CT: AI Press.

Frederick, W. C., ed. 1987. *Research in corporate social performance and policy* pp. 1–23. Greenwich, CT: JAI Press.

Gautschi, F. H., and T. M. Jones. 1987. Illegal corporate behavior and corporate board structure. In W.C. Frederick, ed. *Research in corporate social performance and policy* pp. 93–106. Greenwich, CT: JAI Press.

Goffee, R. & Jones, G. (2000). Why should anyone be led by you? *Harvard Business Review, 78* (5), 62-70. Retrieved October 2, 2002, from Business Source Premier.

Growing the carrot: Encouraging effective corporate compliance. 1996. *Harvard Law Review* 109:1783–1800.

Halcrow, A. 1987. Is there a crisis in business ethics? *Personnel Journal* pp. 10–17.

Hanson, K., and R. Solomon. 1974. The real business ethics. *Business and Society* pp. 41. Retrieved October 9, 2003, from Business Source Premier.

Hill, L., & Wetlaufer, S. (1998) Leadership when there is no one to ask: An interview with Eni's Franco Bernabe. *Harvard Business Review, 76*(4), 80-95. Retrieved October 2, 2002, from Business Source Premier

Hofstede, G. (1980). Motivation, leadership and organization: Do American theories apply abroad. *Organizational Dynamics.* Retrieved April 30, 2003, from Business Source Premier.

Huffington, A. 2003. *Pigs at the trough: How corporate greed and political corruption are undermining America.* New York: Crown.

Joseph, J, and Esen, F. (2003). 2003 Business Ethics Survey (April). Alexandra, VA: Society for Human Resource Management.

Judge W. Q. (2001). Is a leader's character culture-bound or culture-free? An empirical comparison of the character traits of American and Taiwanese CEOs. *Journal of Leadership Studies, 8*(2), 63-79. Retrieved August 15, 2002, from Business Index ASAP.

Kohlberg, L. 1981. *The philosophy of moral development.* New York: Harper and Row.

Labich, K. 1995. Businesses are becoming less ethical. In C. Wekesser, ed. *Ethics* pp.110–115. San Diego, CA: Greenhaven Press.

Lipset, S. M., and R. Schneider. 1983. *The confidence gap: Business, labor and government in the public mind.* New York: The Free Press.

MacLean, T. L. 2001. Thick as thieves: A social embeddedness model rule breaking in organizations. *Business and Society* 40(2):167–196. Retrieved December 7, 2003, from ProQuest.

Mathews, M. C. 1987. Codes of ethics: Organizational behavior and misbehavior. In W.C. Frederick, ed. *Research in corporate social performance and policy* pp. 107–130. Greenwich, CT: JAI Press.

McKendall, M. 1999. Corporate governance and corporate illegality: The effects of board structure on environmental violations. *International Journal of Organizational Analysis* 7(3):201–224. Retrieved November 30, 2003, from Business Source Premier.

McKendall, M. A., and J. A. Wagner. 1997. Motive, opportunity, choice, and corporate illegality. *Organization Science* 8(6):624–647.

McKenna, J.F. (2001). Management in the 21st century: a modest proposal. *Sam Advanced Management Journal,* 4-8. Retrieved October 2, 2002, from Business Source Premier.

New York-Presbysterian. Anatomy of the skin. Retrieved November 24, 2006, from http://wo-pub2.med.cornell.edu.

Nietzsche, F. 1995. Atheism motives people to behave ethically. In C. Wekesser, ed. *Ethics* pp. 23–31. San Diego, CA: Greenhaven Press.

Noddings, N. 1995. A philosophy of caring motives people to behave ethically. In C. Wekesser, ed. *Ethics* pp. 38–46. San Diego, CA: Greenhaven Press.

Pava, M. L, and J. Krausz. 1996. The paradox of social cost. *Journal of Business Ethics* 15(3):321–358. Retrieved August 14, 2003, from ProQuest.

Reidenbach, E. R., and D. P. Robin. 1989. *Business ethics: Where profits meet value systems.* Englewood Cliff, NJ: Prentice Hall.

Rest, J. R. 1979. *Development in judging moral issues.* Minneapolis: University of Minnesota Press.Sidgwick, H. 1873. Utilitarianism. *Utilitas* 12(3):253–260. Retrieved March 11, 2003, from Academic Search Premier.

Simons, T.,L.Pelled, and K.Smith. 1999. Making use of difference: Diversity, debate, and decision comphensiveness in top management teams. *Academy of Management Journal* 42(6):662-673. Retrieved January 6, 2004 from ProQuest.

Society. 1999. *Unethical workers and illegal acts* 36 (May and June): 2–4. Retrieved July 2, 2004 from Academic Premier.

Spencer, M. 1995. *The legal, societal, and management issues.* Westport, CT: Quorum.

Thiroux, J. P. 2001. *Ethics: Theory and practice.* Upper Saddle River, NJ: Prentice Hall.

Thompson, A. A., and A. J. Stickland. 2001. *Strategic Management.* New York: McGraw-Hill Irwin.

Vickers, Mark. n.d. Business ethics and the HR role: Past, present and future. *Human Resource Planning* 28(1):26–31. Retrieved July 30, 2005 from EBSCO.

Victor, B., and J. B. Cullen. 1987. A theory and measure of ethical climate in organizations. In W. C. Frederick, ed. *Research in corporate social performance and policy* pp. 51–71. Greenwich, CT: JAI Press.

Wekesser, C. 1995. *Ethics.* San Diego, CA: Greenhaven Press.

Wimbush, J. C. 1991. Ethical climates and ethical behavior (morality). (UMI *aat 9123764).*